W9-BQY-667

Dynamic
Website Developers

Heather C. Hudak

Checkerboard
Library

An Imprint of Abdo Publishing
abdopublishing.com

ABDOPUBLISHING.COM

Published by Abdo Publishing, a division of ABDO, PO Box 398166, Minneapolis, Minnesota 55439. Copyright © 2019 by Abdo Consulting Group, Inc. International copyrights reserved in all countries. No part of this book may be reproduced in any form without written permission from the publisher. Checkerboard Library™ is a trademark and logo of Abdo Publishing.

Printed in the United States of America, North Mankato, Minnesota
052018
092018

Design: Kelly Doudna, Mighty Media, Inc.
Production: Mighty Media, Inc.
Editor: Liz Salzmann
Cover Photographs: iStockphoto
Interior Photographs: AP Images, pp. 19, 29 (top); Getty Images, p. 11; iStockphoto, pp. 4, 7, 9, 13, 16, 21, 25; John S. and James L. Knight Foundation/Flickr, pp. 15, 28 (bottom); Rama & Musée Bolo/Wikimedia Commons, p. 14; Shutterstock, pp. 23, 27, 29 (bottom)

Library of Congress Control Number: 2017961588

Publisher's Cataloging-in-Publication Data
Name: Hudak, Heather C., author.
Title: Dynamic website developers / by Heather C. Hudak.
Description: Minneapolis, Minnesota : Abdo Publishing, 2019. | Series: It's a digital world! | Includes online resources and index.
Identifiers: ISBN 9781532115325 (lib.bdg.) | ISBN 9781532156045 (ebook)
Subjects: LCSH: Web site development industry--Juvenile literature. | Computer software--Development--Juvenile literature. | Occupations--Careers--Jobs--Juvenile literature.
Classification: DDC 006.7--dc23

CONTENTS

WEBSITES AROUND THE WORLD

It's Sunday afternoon and you've got homework to do. You need to start a report about a world event. You log on to the internet to look for information.

You find a digital database filled with photos and news stories. You watch YouTube video about the event. You take a virtual tour of a display at a national museum. You also find a few books in your library's **online** catalog and put them on hold. When you're done, you play a few online games.

You can do all of these things and much more using websites. There's not much you can't do online, from learning to play an instrument to reading the news. Web developers are the people who create programs and **applications** for the World Wide Web. They are always thinking about new ways to make websites that look great, are easy to use, and have lots of cool features.

CHAPTER 1
FABULOUS FEATURES AND FUNCTIONS

Web developers write the computer programs that make websites work. There are two main types of website development. These are front-end development and back-end development. A developer may do both types. Or he or she may **specialize** in one or the other.

The front end of a website is what users see and experience on the site. This includes what colors different elements are, where buttons are on the page, and more. Front-end web developers often work with web designers. The designers decide how websites should look. Then the developers build the websites.

The back end of a website is how the different features work. This includes forms, shopping carts, search engines, and more. A back-end developer writes the **software** for these functions. He or she makes sure the website works properly for the users.

Web developers like solving problems and building things. Most web developers have a degree in computer science. They take classes in web design and internet security. They also learn about different computer languages, such as HTML, JavaScript, and C++. Website developers keep learning throughout their careers as **technology** changes frequently. They need to keep up with new advancements.

Web development is a growing field. Experts think web developer jobs will increase by 13 percent from 2016 to 2026. This is much faster than other fields!

CHAPTER 2
GETTING DOWN TO BUSINESS

Web developers create websites for different kinds of people and companies. Some companies need websites that promote products and services. Others need websites that describe who they are and what they do. It's the web developer's job to present the company's information **online**. It needs to be nice to look at, be easy to use, and work well.

Before a web developer starts building a website, he or she works with the web designer to gather information. They need to know who will be using the site. How old are they? What interests do they have? This information will guide how the website looks.

The web developer also needs to know how the website will be used. Will people use it to shop online? Should it play videos? Is it a gaming site? The developer thinks about everything a person will be able to do on the website.

Web developers plan websites patiently and pay attention to tiny details.

Once the design of the website is determined, the developer creates a wireframe of the website. This shows how the content and images will be laid out. He or she plans how to build every detail of the design. Then the developer begins building the site. To build a website a developer uses a combination of markup languages and scripts.

CHAPTER 3

MARKUP AND SCRIPTING

Front-end developers use three main languages.
These are HTML, CSS, and JavaScript. *HTML* stands for
"**Hypertext** Markup Language." HTML **code** tells a web
browser what type of content something is. This includes
text, **hyperlinks**, and images.

CSS and JavaScript work with HTML to determine how
websites look. CSS code determines what websites' content
looks like. With CSS, developers program the colors, buttons,
fonts, and more. CSS also lets developers make websites adapt to
different devices and screen sizes. JavaScript is for programming
interactive elements, such as a log-in pages or forms.

Web programming in HTML, CSS, and JavaScript is called
client-side scripting. These programs run in the users' web
browsers. Websites also need to connect to servers to find or
organize information. Back-end web developers build these
elements using server-side scripting.

The programming language Python was created by Dutch computer programmer Guido van Rossum. He named the language after the comedy show *Monty Python's Flying Circus*.

JavaScript can also be used for server-side scripting. Perl, Python, and PHP are other server-side scripting languages. Server-side **code** runs on servers that contain databases of information and images. Programs such as SQL and Oracle manage the databases. Server-side scripts determine how information is transferred between servers and web **browsers**.

CHAPTER 4
WONDERFUL WORKPLACES

Today, most companies have at least one website. They work with one or more web developers to build and maintain their website. Companies of all types and sizes hire web developers.

Some companies are very large. They have thousands of people working for them all over the world. Web developers at these companies are often part of a team. The team members work together to make decisions about the company's websites. Each team member then works on his or her part. This could include creating **graphics**, fixing bugs, or writing **code**.

A smaller company may work with just one web developer. This person is in charge of building and maintaining the company's website. He or she works with others in the company to decide what features the website should have.

Not every company hires web developers directly. Instead they work with companies whose business is developing websites. So, working at a web development company is another type of workplace for web developers.

Some web developers don't work at companies. These developers are freelancers who run their own businesses. They develop websites for many different clients. Sometimes a freelancer may work for a company just on a specific web development project. Some people, such as **bloggers** or celebrities, hire web developers to build their personal websites.

About one in six web developers are self-employed. Many self-employed or freelance developers work from their homes.

CHAPTER 5

BACK IN TIME

Today there are many career paths for website developers. But website developing has only existed for about 25 years. The internet was invented in the 1970s, but it was not **available** to the public at first. There were no websites. The internet was mainly used by the government and universities to transfer data.

In 1989, British computer scientist Tim Berners-Lee got the idea for the World Wide Web (the web). He was

Berners-Lee used a NeXTcube computer for the first web server.

14

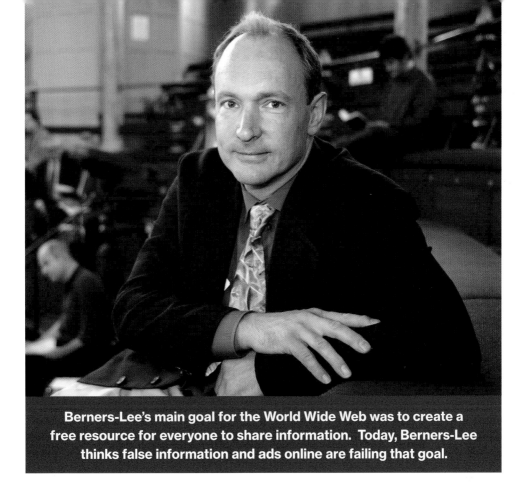

Berners-Lee's main goal for the World Wide Web was to create a free resource for everyone to share information. Today, Berners-Lee thinks false information and ads online are failing that goal.

working at a laboratory known as CERN. Berners-Lee wanted researchers at the lab to be able to share documents with each other on the internet. He created **Hypertext** Transfer Protocol (HTTP). This allowed people to find documents connected by **hyperlinks**.

Over the next year, Berners-Lee invented HTML and programmed the first web server and web **browser**. The web launched at CERN in December 1990. On the first website, Berners-Lee provided information about how to use the web.

CERN was established in 1954. It is located near Geneva, Switzerland, on the border between France and Switzerland.

The web became **available** outside CERN on August 6, 1991. That's when Berners-Lee posted a message in several internet newsgroups. This message explained his web project. It also said how to use HTML to create web pages and transfer them from servers to computers.

On April 30, 1993, CERN made HTML source **code** available to the general public. Anyone in the world could use it to create websites and share information in the internet. Soon, computer scientists began building websites and "web developer" became an official job title.

The web and the internet are often thought to be the same thing, but they are not. The internet is a collection of computers that form interconnected **networks**. The web is a system used to find information on the internet. It consists of web pages. Web pages are documents that are connected by **hyperlinks**. People use web **browsers** to view web pages on the web.

CHAPTER 6
BOOMING BUSINESS

Once the web went public, programmers quickly figured out new ways to design and create websites. Within a few years, websites had progressed beyond text-only pages. They could include images and **graphics**.

In 1993, the web **browser** Mosaic made the web popular among the general public. There were other web browsers, but they looked boring and uninviting. Mosaic had color photos, bookmarks, and more that attracted people to this new way of finding and sharing information.

In 1995, **software** developer Brendan Eich invented JavaScript. Web developers could now add features such as motion and pop-ups to websites. In 1996, David Siegel published the book *Creating Killer Web Sites*. It was the first step-by-step guide for designing and building websites.

In 1998, two major events changed web development and design. First, CSS was improved. CSS had been created in 1994,

Sergey Brin (*left*) and Larry Page (*right*) developed Google while
they were students at Stanford University in California.

but it was difficult to use at first. The problems were fixed and in
1998, it began to be widely used. Then later that year, computer
scientists Larry Page and Sergey Brin launched the Google search
engine. Google changed the way people searched the web. But
this was only the beginning. Website development continued to
grow and change.

CHAPTER 7
GOING MOBILE

In the late 1990s and early 2000s, advancements in website development were mainly driven by better computers. New computers came out that were faster and more powerful. They could run more **complicated** websites.

Then in 2007, Apple released the iPhone. This opened up a whole new world for web developers. Websites designed for computers often didn't work well on **mobile** devices. The sites didn't look good on small screens.

In 2008, web developer Nathan Smith came up with the 960 **grid** system. It divided the screen into columns. This made sketching, designing, and **coding** websites easier. The 960 grid system soon became the standard for most web developers.

Web designer Ethan Marcotte expanded on Smith's grid system to improve mobile websites. At the time, web developers had to build two **versions** of each website. One was for desktop computers and the other for **mobile** devices. In 2010, Marcotte wrote an article describing a solution to this problem.

Marcotte's article explained how to make content formatted in a **grid** display differently on different devices. Marcotte called his idea responsive web design. It greatly simplified the work of developing websites for multiple devices.

Responsive design uses grids and layouts to adjust resolution, image size, and script functions to the device's screen.

CHAPTER 8
FINDING SUCCESS

The most successful web developers do a lot more than just computer programming. These days, many people can learn the basic skills needed to create web pages. A good web developer also needs to understand human interactions. This means knowing how people will use a site and what they want from it. When a site is useful and easy to navigate, people have a better user experience. They will be more likely to come back to the site again.

Successful web developers are good at explaining their ideas. This is helpful when working with clients or coworkers. Developers need to say clearly why a website should have certain features or look a certain way. Developers also need to listen to others' ideas too.

Mark Zuckerberg and several friends came up with the idea for Facebook. They were all students at Harvard University in Massachusetts. They created a website where students could post information and photos.

The website launched on February 4, 2004. It was called The Facebook and at first was only **available** to other Harvard students. The website showed a photo of the students who signed up and listed their contact information. Later that year, Zuckerberg made The Facebook interactive. Students could message each other through the site. And they could post comments on one another's entries.

By the time Facebook became available to the general public in 2006, it also included an **application** programming interface (API). This allowed other programmers to develop apps that worked within Facebook. This revolutionized **social media**. Today, Facebook has more than two billion active monthly users.

CHAPTER 9
SEARCH ENGINE OPTIMIZATION

Having a good website is an important part of any business. But a company can't just launch a website and hope it gets noticed. It's too easy for a website to get lost among the millions of other websites on the web. Having a website won't do any good if people can't find and visit it.

Most possible customers use search engines such as Google, Bing, or Yahoo. For example, someone planning a hiking trip might search for "hiking boots." The search engine shows a list of websites featuring hiking boots. Often, the searcher will only visit the first few sites on the list. So, it's better for a business that sells hiking boots to be at the top of the list.

Web developers help their clients' websites appear high on search engine lists. This is called search engine **optimization** (SEO). How a developer builds a website affects its SEO ranking. Websites that load slowly tend to have low rankings. Elements such as large images can make websites slow.

People can use software or apps to track their SEO ranking and website traffic. One popular tracking service is Google Analytics.

Websites that only work well on one or two types of devices also have low rankings. Web developers try to build strong, fast websites for computers and **mobile** devices. This ensures that their websites will have high SEO rankings.

CHAPTER 10

TARGETING TRENDS

SEO is just one element that is making websites more complicated to design and build. The web is always changing and growing. Web developers need to be able to keep up with the latest trends so they can build better websites.

Virtual reality (VR) is an emerging trend in website development. VR creates an artificial setting that users can move around in and interact with. Developers are working on ways to include VR on websites. One idea is to use VR to connect people **online** so they can interact and even play games.

Another trend is the Internet of Things (IoT). It is the ability of objects such as household **appliances**, music systems, and cars to connect online. This includes refrigerators that tell you when you need to buy more milk. And some cars, such as Teslas, can receive **software** updates directly from the manufacturer. Web developers need to be able to build sites that can exchange information with devices that are on the IoT.

When there are safety issues with a Tesla car, the car can receive an update that fixes the problem!

Web developers are always being faced with new challenges. **Technology** changes so quickly that it is impossible to know what the future holds for the web. One thing is sure, though. Website developers will help shape the way people communicate, make decisions, and perform daily tasks.

TIMELINE

1993
HTML source code becomes available to the general public. The Mosaic web browser is created.

1996
David Siegel publishes *Creating Killer Websites*.

1970s
The internet is invented.

1989
Tim Berners-Lee starts developing the World Wide Web.

1995
Brendan Eich invents JavaScript.

1998
The Google search engine is launched.

2004
Mark Zuckerberg launches The Facebook at Harvard University.

2006
Facebook becomes available to everyone.

2007
Apple releases the first iPhone.

2008
Nathan Smith invents the 960 grid system.

2010
Ethan Marcotte writes an article explaining responsive web design.

GLOSSARY

appliance–a household or office device operated by gas or electric current. Common kitchen appliances include stoves, refrigerators, and dishwashers.

application–a computer program.

available–able to be had or used.

blogger–someone who maintains a type of website called a blog that tells about his or her personal opinions, activities, and experiences.

browser–a computer program that is used to find and look at information on the Internet.

code–a set of instructions for a computer. Writing code is called coding.

complicated–having elaborately combined parts.

graphics–pictures or images on the screen of a computer, smartphone, or other device.

grid–a pattern with rows of squares, such as a checkerboard.

hyperlink–an electronic element that provides access between pieces of information. The information can be accessed by clicking a computer mouse on the hyperlink.

hypertext–a computer system that allows users to access information connected to what is on screen.

mobile–capable of moving or being moved.

network–a system of computers connected by communications lines.

online–connected to the internet.

optimization–the act, process, or method of making something as functional or effective as possible.

social media–forms of electronic communication that allow people to create online communities to share information, ideas, and messages. Facebook, Instagram, and Snapchat are examples of social media.

software–the written programs used to operate a computer.

specialize–to pursue one type of work, called a specialty.

technology (tehk-NAH-luh-jee)–machinery and equipment developed for practical purposes using scientific principles and engineering.

version–a different form or type of an original.

INDEX